Wonderful, Wonderful Copenhagen!
A Kid's Guide To Copenhagen, Denmark

Photography By John D. Weigand
Poetry By Penelope Dyan

Bellissima Publishing, LLC
Jamul, California
www.bellissimapublishing.com

copyright © 2011 by Penny D. Weigand and John D. Weigand

All rights reserved. No part of this book may be reproduced or transmitted in any form or by any means, electronic or mechanical, including photocopying, recording, or by any other means, or by any information or storage retrieval system, without permission from the publisher.

ISBN 978-1-935630-62-3

First Edition

*To the late Julius Petersen,
who never forgot the little mermaid,
even though he was far, far from home.*

Wonderful, Wonderful Copenhagen
Bellissima Publishing, LLC

Introduction

Han's Christian Andersen said, "Every man's life is a fairy tale, written by God's fingers." And if we begin as empty slates for God to write upon, then this is what must have happened to Hans Christian Andersen! Now you can walk where he walked and see what he saw and find out what motivated him and inspired him to be a great writer.

John D. Weigand and Penelope Dyan traveled to this magical place to see where all the inspiration began and to experience the serene beauty of this place they call 'Wonderful, Wonderful Copenhagen.' Kid's can use this book when they travel to Copenhagen and insert pictures, tickets and notes, and make up their very own fairy-tales to tell to their friends when they get home! Or they can travel vicariously with Dyan and Weigand through the pages of this book.

Written by award winning author, Penelope Dyan to complement the beautiful photography of John D. Weigand, this book serves several purposes, one of which is to enlarge the horizons of the young. Use this book as you talk about one very famous author, Hans Christian Andersen, so that your child may see where this man lived and what inspired him. Ater all, all kids know his stories!

Besides being an award winning author, Penelope Dyan is also an attorney and a former teacher. She brings her teaching expertise to the table with every book she writes. And when a child recognizes what he has already seen in a book, traveling can be ever so much more delightful and exciting!

Wonderful, Wonderful Copenhagen
Bellissima Publishing, LLC

Wonderful, Wonderful Copenhagen!
A Kid's Guide To Copenhagen, Denmark

Photography By John D. Weigand
Poetry By Penelope Dyan

In Copenhagen, Denmark there is a place
everyone knows quite well.
And that well known place is the Nyhavn Canal.
From the seventeenth century
it has existed in this city.
It is a well known site that is very, very pretty.
And the children here are all quiet, I hear tell,
and they ALL behave extremely well.

Down the canal you can float,
with a tour guide on a boat.
And they will tell wonderful stories to you.
And they will answer all your questions too!
And when the boat ride is over and done
you will say to them, "That sure was fun!"

There is so much color and beauty you can see,
where Hans Christian Andersen's home
once used to be.
You can imagine him walking down the street,
creating a story in his head, not skipping a beat.
When you are here maybe you will write a story,
about kings, and queens and palaces of glory.
And when at night you go to sleep in your bed,
mermaids and kings will dance in your head.

There are loads of shops and places to eat.
You can even buy pastry flaky and sweet.
There are delicious hot dogs there.
But NO Danish sausages, to this I swear!*
And if it's an ebelskiver you want to eat,
you'll wait for Christmas for that special treat.

*Apparently, Danish sausage is an item unique to Solvang, California, USA as the author and photographer did go in search for it.

You can see the palace standing large and tall.
In its majesty you may feel small.

As the guards change places. watch their feet.
marching in step, they don't miss a beat.
(You will correctly think that it must be hard,
to do the changing of the palace guard.)

You can see the little mermaid sitting on a rock.
Around Tivoli Gardens you can take a walk.
As the mermaid sits as serenely as can be,
you'll think about the mermaids in the living sea.
And you can read this mermaid's story
(if you want to take a look)
into Hans Christian Andersen's FAMOUS
fairy-tale book!

You can take a ride on a carousel
and you'll have LOTS of fun,
As you run all around Tivoli Gardens
in the noon day's sun.

On the Tivoli Gardens' carousel
you can smile, wave and laugh,
As you share a ride with your sister
on a VERY tall giraffe!

And this brown bear may even do a dance,
in his royal blue hat and red polka dotted pants!

You'll ride in a plane that goes upside down.
Your knees will wobble when you're on the ground.

Then too soon you'll leave Copenhagen
and you'll be on your way.
But you will come back to visit someday.
Because once this place is in your heart,
from wonderful Copenhagen you'll never part!

"Just living is not enough," said the butterfly, "one must have sunshine, freedom, and a little flower."

Hans Christian Andersen

www.ingramcontent.com/pod-product-compliance
Ingram Content Group UK Ltd.
Pitfield, Milton Keynes, MK11 3LW, UK
UKHW060136240426
12048UKWH00002B/55